# Grandmother
by
Linda D.Spivey

© 1997 Havoc Publishing
ISBN 1-57977-109-2

Published by Havoc Publishing
San Diego, California

First printing, May 1997

Design © 1997 under license from Penny Lane Publishing, Inc.

Printed in China

Please write to us for more information on our Havoc Publishing
Record Books and Products.

HAVOC PUBLISHING

6330 Nancy Ridge Drive, Suite 104

San Diego, California 92121

I dedicate this book to my
Mother, Rose Mary
the Grandmother of my sons.
With Love,
Linda
♡

~ Wednesday's child is full of Woe ~ Thursday's Child has far to go ~

Born This Day

———— DATE - TIME ————

———— NAME ————

———— WEIGHT ~ LENGTH ————

The Proud Parents

Monday's Child is fair of face ~ Tuesday's child is full of grace ~

Friday's Child is loving and giving ~ Saturday's Child works hard for a living ~

And a Child born on the Sabbath day is fair and wise and good and gay.

Grandma, tell me about when and where you were born. _____
_____
_____
_____
_____
_____

Do you know why you were given the name you have?
_____
_____
_____

What events happened the year you were born?_____
_____
_____
_____

Grandma, tell me about your mother. What is her full name and when and where was she born? Where did she grow up? Any interesting stories about her?

_____

_____

_____

_____

_____

_____

_____

_____

_____

_____

May Love be the ♡ of this Home

Tell me Grandma about your Father. What is his full name and when and where was he born? Where did he grow up? What did he do for a living? Any interesting stories about your Father? _____

_____

_____

_____

_____

_____

_____

Home is Where they love you

_____

_____

_____

_____

_____

_____

Family Photographs

Grandmother, tell me about your brothers and sisters. What are their full names and birthdates. _____

_____

_____

_____

_____

Did you share a room with anyone? Tell about this.

_____

_____

_____

_____

_____

_____

Grandma, tell me about your Grandparents. What are their
full names, where were they born? What do you remember
about them?    Your Mother's mother: _____

_____

_____

_____

_____

Your Mother's father: _____

_____

_____

_____

_____

_____

Your Father's mother: _____
_____
_____
_____
_____
_____
_____

Your Father's father: _____
_____
_____
_____
_____
_____
_____
_____

Photographs

Loving is Caring ~ Caring is Sharing ~ Sharing is Living
Living is Loving ~ Loving is Caring

L.Spivey ©

When you were young Grandmother, how did you celebrate Valentines Day? Did you have school parties? _____

_____

_____

_____

_____

_____

_____

Did you ever make a Valentine for someone special? Who did you give it to? _____

_____

_____

_____

_____

Grandma, did you have a special quilt or blanket? Who
made it? _____

_____

_____

_____

_____

Did you learn how to sew or knit? Who taught you?

_____

_____

_____

_____

Did you ever enter anything at the County Fair?

_____

_____

_____

Grandma, do you have any Springtime memories? Did you ever fly a Kite? Who made the Kite?_____

_____

_____

_____

_____

_____

_____

What do you remember about your childhood home and neighborhood?_____

_____

_____

_____

_____

_____

_____

_____

What memories do you have Grandma, of going to church as a child? _____

_____

_____

_____

_____

Did you go to an Easter Sunrise Service? _____

_____

_____

_____

Tell about your family Easter traditions. Did you have Easter egg hunts? _____

_____

_____

_____

_____

Grandma, did you have a very
favorite doll or teddy bear?
Who gave it to you? Did
your doll have a name?

_____

_____

_____

_____

_____

_____

What ever became of it?_____

_____

_____

_____

Did you have any favorite games you liked to play?

_____

_____

Summer
time
Solace

Grandma, what was your favorite activity in the summer? How did you keep cool? _____

_____

_____

_____

Did you ride a bike? Where would you ride to? _____

_____

_____

Did you ever go camping? Where did you go? _____

_____

_____

_____

All creatures great and small, the Lord God made them all...........

Grandmother, when you were young did you have a favorite pet? Tell me about him/her. What was a funny thing they did? _____

_____

_____

_____

_____

_____

_____

_____          ☆ Photo of Pet ☆

_____

_____

_____

_____

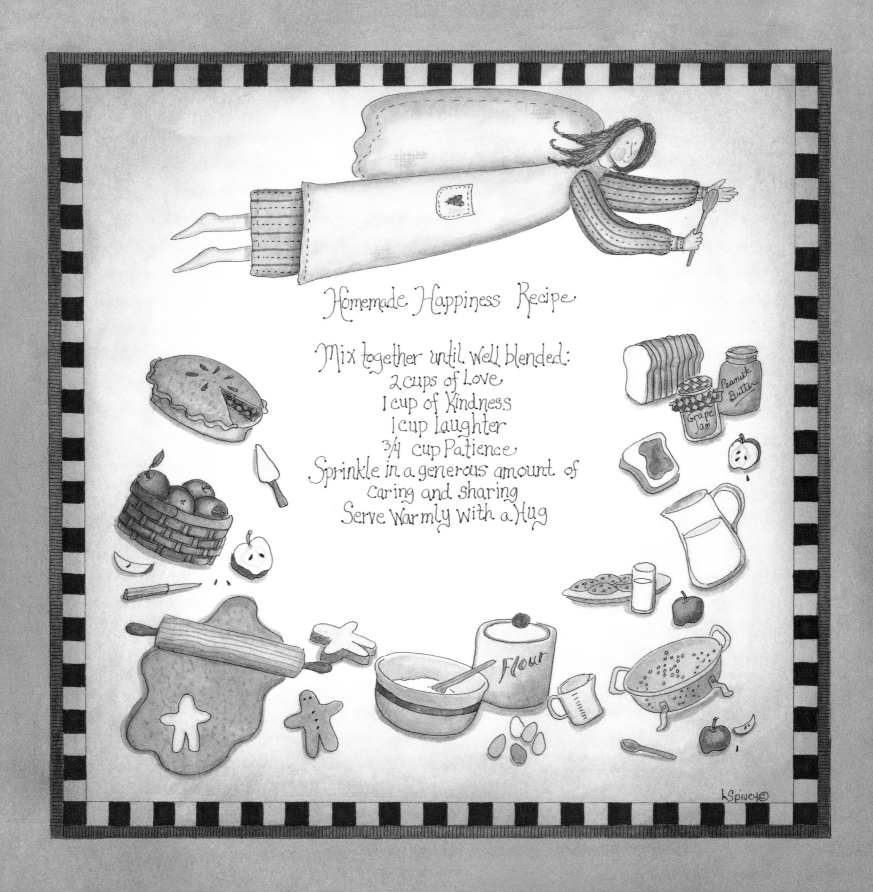

Homemade Happiness Recipe

Mix together until well blended:
2 cups of Love
1 cup of Kindness
1 cup Laughter
3/4 cup Patience
Sprinkle in a generous amount of
caring and sharing
Serve Warmly with a Hug

Grandma, when you were young, what did you do to help in the Kitchen? _____

_____

_____

What other chores were you expected to do around the house?

_____

_____

_____

Was your mother a very good cook? What Kind of food did she fix most of the time? _____

_____

_____

_____

_____

# Family Favorite Recipes

# Family Favorite Recipes

Grandma, what schools did you attend?_____

_____

_____

_____

_____

_____

_____

What was your favorite subject?_____

_____

_____

Did you have any special teachers? How did they influence
you?_____

_____

_____

_____

APPLES 5¢

What would you do at Recess time?

_____

_____

_____

_____

Were you ever in a school play?_____

_____

_____

_____

_____

Did you ever go on a school trip?_____

_____

_____

_____

_____

_____

Tell me about your High School days. What year did you graduate? How many were in your graduating class? Tell me about graduation day. _____

_____

_____

_____

_____

Did you go to your Prom or a big dance? Who with? Tell me about it. _____

_____

_____

_____

_____

What were your school colors and mascot? _____

_____

_____

_____

School Pictures

School Pictures

Grandma, did you play any sports in school? How good were you?

_____

_____

_____

_____

_____

_____

Did you go to school sports events? What were your favorites? _____

_____

_____

_____

Did you play an instrument, were you in the Band?

_____

_____

_____

Within the Garden of my heart,
the flowers of friendship grow.
It is blossoms of Remembrance,
to keep my Heart Aglow.

Grandma, tell me about your best friends in school when young. What did you do together? _____

_____

_____

_____

_____

_____

Who were your best friends in High School? What was the best thing you did together? _____

_____

_____

_____

_____

_____

Grandma, when you were a young girl, did you go Trick-Or-Treating on Halloween? What did you dress up as? Where did you get your costumes? _____

_____

_____

_____

_____

Did you carve a pumpkin? Did you make scary faces or happy face pumpkins? _____

_____

_____

_____

What kind of treats did you get? _____

_____

_____

Grandma, how did your family celebrate Thanksgiving when you were young? Did you have guests?

_____

_____

_____

_____

_____

_____

_____

_____

What foods were served? Who did all the cooking?

_____

_____

_____

# Special Holiday Recipes

# Special Holiday Recipes

There's no place like home for the Holidays

Grandma, tell me how your family celebrated Christmas when you were a child. Did you hang up a stocking for Santa to fill?

_____

_____

_____

_____

_____

_____

_____

_____

What kind of gifts did you give your Mother and Father. Did Your mother ever make you something very special?

_____

_____

_____

_____

_____

Grandma, tell me about the biggest winter storm you experienced.

_____

_____

_____

_____

_____

Did you ever go sledding or ice skating? Who did you do
this with? _____

_____

_____

_____

_____

_____

Did you build a snowman or snow fort? _____

_____

_____

Grandma, tell me all about Grandpa. How old were you and he when you met? What did you like about him? _____

_____

_____

_____

_____

What did you do together on dates? How long did you date before you got married? _____

_____

_____

_____

_____

What did your parents think of him? _____

_____

What is Grandpa's full name? Where and when was he born? _____

_____

_____

What are the names of his brother and sisters? _____

_____

_____

What are the full names of his Mother and Father? Do you know where they were born and grew up? _____

_____

_____

_____

What did Grandpa do for a living? _____

_____

Did Grandpa serve in the Military? Tell me about this.

_____

_____

_____

_____

Tell me about your Wedding day. When and where did
you get married. Who married you? Did you wear a
special dress? Where did you get your dress? Cost?

_____

_____

_____

_____

_____

_____

_____

_____

Where was your first home together, you and Grandpa?

_____

_____

_____

When did you start a family? Tell me about when
you had my parent? What were they like as a baby, child,
teenager? _____

_____

_____

_____

_____

_____

_____

_____

_____

Photographs

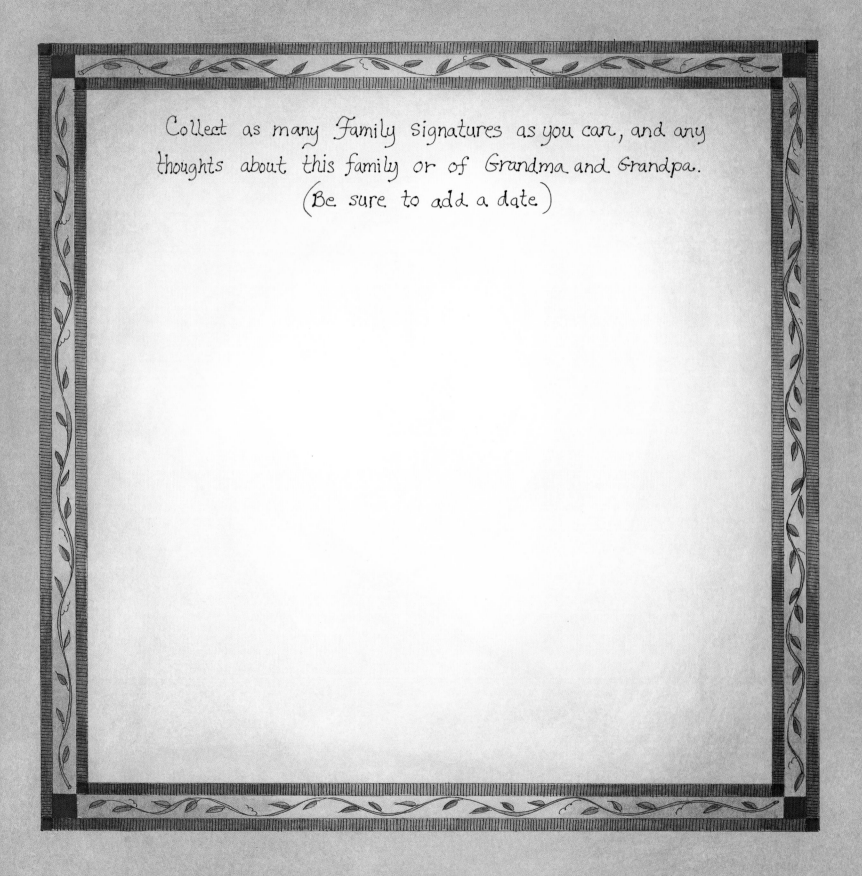

Collect as many Family signatures as you can, and any thoughts about this family or of Grandma and Grandpa.
(Be sure to add a date)

Family Signatures

# Family Signatures

# Available Record Books
# from Havoc

Animal Antics-Cats
Animal Antics-Dogs
Couples
Girlfriends
Golf
Grandmother
Honeymoon
Mom
Sisters
Tying the Knot
Traveling Adventures

Please write to us with your ideas for additional
Havoc Publishing Record Books and Products

HAVOC PUBLISHING

6330 Nancy Ridge Drive, Suite 104

San Diego, California 92121